20 Seconds

Neal and Alisa Grandy

Copyright © 2013 Acacia Holdings LLC

All rights reserved.

ISBN:0989880222
ISBN-13: 978 0 9898802 2 0

Photo Credits:

Kirill Kurashov, Cover
Chris Kotsiopoulous, pg. 7
Matt Bradbury, pg. 10
NASA, pg. 18
Petar Sabol, pg. 29
Rodney Hyett, pg. 41
Anup Shah & Fiona Rogers, pg.47
David Nightingale, pg. 62
Babasteve, pg. 70

Baloncici, TOC, pgs. 3,20
Stanko Mravljak, pg. 8
Claude Nicollier, pg. 16
Yuryy Bezrukov, pg. 22
AP, pgs. 30,31,32
Vadim Trunov, pg. 44
Coy Aune, pg. 55
Brenda Carson, pg. 67
Maigi, pg. 80

D1731044

20 Seconds
Table of Contents

How much time do you have?

Improve someone's outlook. . .

Make someone's day. . .

Change someone's life. . .

You have the power.

It only takes. . .

20 Seconds

20 seconds is all it takes to make a difference in somebody's life. It's a small investment that all leaders can make to show their people how valuable they are.

20 Seconds?

How can you have an impact on *anything* in just 20 seconds?

20 seconds is nothing. . .

It's four or five average blinks of an eye, a couple of at rest breaths.

It's a wisp, a snippet, a flicker of a candle.

Nothing happens in just 20 seconds. . .

Or does it?

20 seconds is one tenth of a lifetime for certain Mayflies.

20 seconds for you is about 0000005% of your lifetime.

In 20 seconds, a hummingbird in flight
flaps its wings over a thousand times
and its heart beats 420 times.

In 20 seconds, **you** can brush your upper teeth.

In 20 seconds, the fastest land animal
on the planet can cover nearly
a third of a mile.

In 20 seconds, you can move from your sofa to the kitchen. Twice.

In 20 seconds the earth rotates nearly six miles at the equator.

In 20 seconds, you can read the latest tweet. And respond. Twice.

It takes about 20 seconds for the sun to set when viewed from space…

It took 200 thousand years for us to *get* to space.

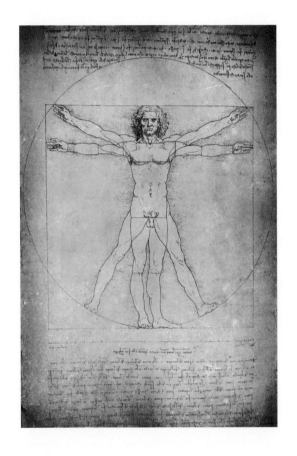

On July 20, 1969, at 4:17:40 pm EDT, the crew of Apollo 11 landed the lunar module, Eagle, on the surface of the moon. The chosen landing site was known as Mare Tranquillitatas--The Sea of Tranquility. In the final minutes of the descent, Commander Neil Armstrong had to manually pilot the Eagle in order to avoid a crater 180 meters across and 30 meters deep.

After some rather tense moments, they were finally able to safely land the module--6 kilometers west of the original planned landing site. They had approximately 20 seconds of fuel left...

"You know, sometimes all you need is 20 seconds of insane courage. Just literally 20 seconds of just embarrassing bravery. And I promise you, something great will come of it."

Benjamin Mee, We Bought A Zoo

Sometimes 20 seconds can mean the difference between success and failure. In the grand scheme of things however, it really is just an instant in the average life span of nearly every creature on the planet.

So given our own limitations as one of those creatures, and most particularly as time-pressed managers and leaders, what can *we* possibly accomplish in just 20 seconds?

We can improve someone's outlook…

We can make someone's day…

We can change someone's life…

And in so doing, we can
change our own.

The 20 Second Rule

Single out an individual in your organization and give them 20 seconds of your time. That's it. That's the rule. A mere 20 seconds… In that 20 seconds your job is to praise, to acknowledge, to enable, and to motivate. Seems like a tall order for such a short amount of time, doesn't it? How do you do all that in just 20 seconds? The first step is simple:

single out an individual.

The 20 Second Rule is all about making a brief but very real connection with someone in particular. It's not about strolling through a department, slapping folks on the back, and saying "good job" to everyone you come across. It is person specific and performance, activity, or event specific.

Specificity is the rule.

Call that individual by name, cite the particular instance of job performance, and personalize the accomplishment. It can range from something as simple as a routine task done well to something completely outside the scope of an individual's responsibilities. You're recognizing good behavior, and you're letting them know it. That recognition can take many forms: an email, a long handshake, a quick comment, a phone call, a handwritten note. You can even shout it out in a meeting of their peers.

Just make it:
task/performance/behavior

specific.

And make it personal.

20 seconds is all about *that* individual. Your desires, your goals, your needs as a manager don't come into play. Any hidden agenda that you allow to creep into the process undermines everything you are trying to achieve. A compliment for compliment's sake is not the goal. People can spot insincerity and they have a keen sense of when they are being manipulated. So you can't simply play the role or fake the process; you must believe it and feel it. Be honest, enthusiastic and open. Find that place within yourself that makes you want to do it. That's the only way it will work.

It is better to never use the rule
then to use it badly.

Praise

Acknowledge

Enable

Motivate

"There are two things that people want more than sex or money...recognition and praise."
Mary Kay Ash, Distinguished Texas Cosmetician

"I can live for two months on a good compliment."
Mark Twain, Mississippi River Boat Pilot/Humorist

No Room For Buts

Critiquing and correcting performance is a process unto itself and as such, is a management task that should be clearly segregated. Obviously, periodic reviews and evaluations should incorporate a balanced discussion of achievements and shortcomings, however, the 20 Second Rule is all about your brief, *daily* interactions. It is completely *unbalanced* precisely because it is focused exclusively on positive feedback.

Addressing performance deficiencies should have no place, then, when using your 20 seconds. Praising someone in such a short time frame is actually minimized if it is followed by however.

Think of the 20 Second Rule as your one and only, completely unbalanced managerial tool.

Occasionally you may have the desire to circumvent the rule and substitute the word And for But:

"This is excellent work, and I think we're just about there. One more push and we've got it. Well done."

This may achieve your desired results but clearly depends on your corporate culture, the people involved, and the amount of trust they feel. This type of exchange clearly bends the rule and should be used sparingly, if at all. You want your people to buy in to your vision, and charging them extra can backfire.

It is better to never use the rule
then to use it badly.

*"Character is like a tree and reputation like a shadow. The
shadow is what we think of it; the tree is the real thing."*
Abraham Lincoln, American Abolitionist

On a cold and snowy afternoon on January 13, 1982, Air Florida Flight 90 smashed into the 14th Street Bridge in Washington D. C. The plane struck seven vehicles and then careened nose first into the ice-packed Potomac River below. Half the fuselage disappeared in an instant.

Of the 79 people on board, only six survived, and they found themselves in the middle of the frigid river clinging to the wreckage of what used to be the tail section. Although they were only about fifty feet from shore, the floating ice and biting cold water made it virtually impossible for anyone to get to them, although one brave man, Roger Olian, tried repeatedly.

An agonizing twenty minutes passed, and as the six began to succumb to hypothermia, the situation looked hopeless. At last a small Park Service helicopter arrived on the scene. The crew lowered a lifeline and began lifting the survivors from the water.

Three people were pulled to safety. Of the three remaining, one was still on the tail, and two were now in the water, Priscilla Tirado and Nikki Felch. Only Felch was wearing a life jacket, so the helicopter crew made the attempt to reach Tirado. She was able to grab the lifebelt attached to the line but no longer had the strength to hold on. Twice she slipped away. The effects of hypothermia now clearly visible, her strength completely sapped, disoriented and buffeted by the chop of the water, she slipped under the surface. She popped up and then slipped under again.

The crowd, watching from the river bank, were helpless, horrified, seemingly mesmerized by the event unfolding before them. Among them was a man named Lenny Skutnik who just happened to be on his way home from work that afternoon. As he watched Priscilla Tirado drowning just thirty feet away, he could stand no more. He yanked off his parka and boots, plunged into the icy water, and reached her. The time between Lenny's decision to plunge into that freezing water up to the moment he was finally able to push Priscilla into the helping hands of others on shore took just about 20 seconds.

20 seconds of just embarrassing bravery.

Two weeks later Lenny Skutnik was honored by President Ronald Reagan at that year's State of the Union address.

This story is not meant to suggest that you should risk your life in the pursuit of personal and/ or organizational goals. Often, however, it does require some bravery to change the way you do things. Like Lenny, you need to choose a bold course of action, fully commit to it, and see it through. It takes courage to step out of your comfort zone and manage things in a different way.

"You've got to go out on a limb sometimes because that's where the fruit is."
Will Rogers, Social Commentator and Anti-Bunk Party Leader

If you're feeling stuck, changing the way you interact with people is a great place to start. Initially this can be difficult; changing your entire management style is even more so. But if you're doing things the same way and rarely getting the results you want, then what other choice do you have?

The 20 Second Rule can ease the way. It can simplify many communication related aspects of your job and eventually it may even allow you to transition into a completely new and more effective managerial style.

Stalking Performance

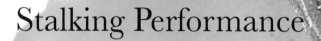

*"Help people reach their full potential. Catch
them doing something right."*
Ken Blanchard, Time-constrained
Management Guru

A management task that gets
overlooked in many organizations is the
simple act of looking for good behavior.
Searching for people doing things right
is absolutely at the heart of the 20
Second Rule. Managers and supervisors
everywhere either do not embrace this
concept or are completely unaware of
it. As a result, there is a nearly
pathological quest in many
organizations to stalk bad behavior. The
consequences are fairly predictable:
average performance, low morale, high
turnover and a cowed workforce.

*"If you only have a hammer, you tend to see
every problem as a nail."*
Abraham Maslow, Self-actualized Psychologist

Too many managers spend their time looking for and documenting bad behavior. If this is your focus, how can you possibly see anything else? Your search for sub-par performance creates tunnel vision--it narrows your perception and it forces your workforce to keep their heads down.

Strong managers want people on their teams who hold their heads high, who are proud of the work they do, and who are eager to show it. That is the kind of workplace atmosphere that allows people to excel. For those of you trapped in the hunt for inadequacies, you are simply wasting valuable time.

Sub-par performance always reveals itself; you rarely have to look that hard for it. So if you're stuck on that treadmill, attempt to spend a few minutes a day breaking the cycle--seek out and compliment positive behavior. If you do this consistently, people throughout the organization will start to see it and even the poor performers will want a piece.

Stalking performance leads to stockpiling performance...

"I think it is an immutable law in business that words are words, explanations are explanations, promises are promises--but only performance is reality."
Harold S. Geneen, CEO ITT Corp.
Conglometer Extraordinaire

Once you begin to eliminate the plethora of negativity in your day, managing becomes so much easier. By focusing on the positive and constantly reinforcing it, you suddenly find yourself marginalizing the negative. Eventually you may find that you don't even have to respond to sub-par performance. Once you have established a consistent pattern of acknowledgment and recognition, people instantly know that their work is not up to par when you say nothing. When you say nothing! And that silence can be a monster of a motivator. As time goes by, people begin to see the pattern, they want that recognition, and they know what they must do in order to get it.

"For some reason, there never seems to be enough recognition. After a brutal day, walk up to employees and say, 'You were great. I'm so glad about what you did today.' You'll be surprised how far a simple gesture will go."
Robert Preziosi, Leader, trainer, and educator
of leaders, trainers, and educators

Ward Clapham of the Royal Canadian Mounted Police in Richmond, BC, had a difficult job. He was paid to catch people acting badly. Poor performance was his reason for being. But Mr. Clapham understood the flip side of that coin, and in fact went out of his way to embrace it. His goal was to change the perception on the street "that kids were the prey and he was the hunter." Mr. Clapham began to hand out what he called "Positive Tickets" to at-risk kids all over town. These citations entitled the recipient to a free meal, or a show, or admittance to a theme park. The purpose was to look for kids who were doing something right, small things like cleaning up a park, helping an elderly person with groceries, or simply staying in school. Positive youth development--that was the objective. Mr. Clapham and his associates handed out thousands of these tickets as a way to reinforce good behavior, and as a result, the entire community benefited.

Remember when you were a kid and how it felt to be complimented by a teacher? You felt warm and nearly giddy. You threw your shoulders back, stood a little taller, felt a bit of pride. 20 seconds is about channeling that inner 6-year-old in us all, the child who always performs better for having his or her name up in proverbial lights.

What Is Your Leadership Wake?

"The brain is a wonderful organ; it starts working the moment you get up in the morning and does not stop until you get into the office."
Robert Frost, Pulitzer Winning Poetic Farmer

Many of us get up in the morning and go about our daily routine with the notion that our professional lives are fairly mundane and unexciting. In our minds, we don't really matter in the grand scheme of the organization and so we chug along, doing what we have to in a competent but rather uninspired way. We believe that we're just another cog in the machine. Often, we're right. We're not that important.

Our employees however, think otherwise, not because of who we are personally, but because of where we are professionally. Our relative standing absolutely matters to them!

You know that your employees talk about you. They talk among themselves, with their friends after work, and with their families around the dinner table at home. What do you think they say? What do you hope they say?

Every interaction you have with your employees is a reflection of your leadership wake. Even when you are just passing through, you make these waves. Your mere presence can raise the anxiety level of the workforce and you might not even be aware of it. Remember:

Your level of stress is absolutely transferable.

Before you step into that department
or out onto that sales floor, think about
the kind of disruption you have the
ability to cause. . .

"If you could kick the person in the pants responsible for most of your trouble, you wouldn't sit for a month."
Theodore Roosevelt, Adventurous Nobel Laureate

As a leader, you have complete control over the quality of your daily disruptions. You have complete control over how you insert yourself into someone's day. It *can* and *should* be a positive experience, even if you're shaking things up.

If everyone seems to be just going through the motions, overturning the metaphorical applecart may be just what the doctor ordered. A little positive disruption, even on a small scale, often yields something great.

Practice some positive disruption.
It just might make everyone's day. . .

A newly promoted manager attended his first big staff meeting. He was a little nervous because this was the first meeting not only with his new peer group, but also with a number of high-level company executives. He really didn't know what to expect, but based on the somber looks of some of the higher-ups, it was looking like it might get brutal. The meeting was just about to get underway, when suddenly the doors flew open and in stepped a gorilla wearing a pink tutu, bearing a singing telegram. Just a few seconds of positive disruption to welcome a new leader.

Many managers are unhappy with the goals they have set in terms of employee performance and never seriously consider the possibility that the problem lies with themselves. The connection between poor employee performance and poor employee management is lost on scores of otherwise bright people in leadership positions.

And much of the problem resides in how they communicate. They rarely think about, let alone examine, the quality of their brief exchanges with their associates. They are dismissive, confrontational, and insecure. This is communicated quite clearly, even if they never utter a word.

A team member sought my approval for a proposed project. In turn, I submitted the request to my boss via email for his approval. My boss responded with one word, 'approved.' I was about to send the identical one-word email back to the team member when I realized that a blunt one word response seemed almost. . . dismissive. It was so curt that it nearly sounded like no, even though it was yes! Somehow, I could have a better impact. . . And then it hit me. The email I sent read, 'Approved. Congratulations!' One extra word to convey my support and enthusiasm. The team member's response was immediate, ecstatic, and accompanied by a number of additional suggestions. It took just a few seconds to entirely change the tone of that brief exchange.

Unfortunately, many organizations neglect the power of positivism. It often seems that in our quest for efficiency, we tend to eliminate many of the characteristics and human qualities that make work enjoyable. We don't have the time or we don't use it wisely. In addition, leaders sometimes get so caught up in their own sense of power that they forget just who it is they are leading.

As a manager, your people come to you every day with all kinds of requests. They ask for approval, for permission, for assistance and for recognition.

Find a way to yes.

Or modify your no. Even a denial of a request can result in a positive exchange if you simply alter the message.

*Say yes because you should,
instead of no
because you can.*

Effective leadership is about empowerment.
Give your people a job, the tools and the
authority to get it done, and then get out of the
way. Allow and encourage them to find their
own solutions to problems and obstacles. People
want that autonomy. It is their responsibility and
they should feel that they own it. Let them.

There are only two instances when you
should step back in. The first is when it is not
going well or, worse, the job is not getting done
at all, in which case the time you spend dealing
with it could be measured in hours or days. The
second is when it *is* going well and the time you
spend praising and encouraging is measured in
seconds.

About 20 of them should just about do it.

*"Managing is getting paid for home runs
that someone else hits."*
Casey Stengel, 'Perfessorial' Hall of Famer

This means, of course, that we need to let go of our egos. We have to trust the people we work with. And we absolutely must fight the innate desire to micro-manage. That in and of itself is a motivation killer because it eliminates nearly every opportunity for someone else to shine. In environments like that, the best performers leave and those that remain hope they don't get fired. The workplace has an atmosphere of fear and intimidation.

Sometimes, when pulled in all directions by the demands placed upon them, managers can fall prey to a host of negative behaviors. And they can unwittingly allow a process of manipulation and dishonesty to creep into their daily interactions. This might occur even among those who understand and practice the 20 Second Rule. In cases like this, it is not just the rule which is undermined, it is the trust of the employee. And once that is lost, all is lost. . . You never get that back!

Put yourself into your employees' shoes. Respond to them and they'll respond to you. Be where they are, instead of where you are. They should know exactly what is expected of them and what they can expect from you.

The bottom line is this:

You get the staff you deserve.

The brief exchanges you have throughout the day--voiced or not--speak volumes. What is the message you send? When is the last time you acknowledged someone on the front lines you don't even know with a nod and a smile? When is the last time you gave someone a metaphorical high-five? A fast email to an associate in reply to a routine report? Or simply stopped someone to shake their hand?
When is the last time you just said thank you?

Think about your leadership wake. You have the power to lift up so many boats, as well as the power to swamp them. . .

Why Are You Waiting For the Annual Performance Review?

Like most managerial techniques, the 20 Second Rule is a process. It takes time and effort. You have to pay attention, document and track performance, think about a tailored response. The simple act of catching people doing something right is often not that simple. To be effective, the 20 Second Rule takes far more time than you might like. . .

"Do the difficult things while they are easy and do the great things while they are small. A journey of a thousand miles must begin with a single step."
Lao Tzu, Libertarian Taoist

A manager with a large retail chain was meeting with one of his front line supervisors for her annual review. The first thing he did was pull out a file that documented nearly every accomplishment she had made in the last year. These achievements were not just the job metrics, but included subjective items like team building, problem solving, and conflict resolution. Specific instances and results were cited.

Naturally the supervisor was surprised and could not believe this manager had not only taken the time to notice these subjective accomplishments, but made the effort to note them and then present them to her.

The 20 Second Rule is exactly about making this kind of impact. The supervisor was ecstatic to get that kind of feedback.

And she only had to wait a year!

That's only 31,536,000 seconds.

Why are you waiting for the annual performance review?

The 20 Second Rule should be used often and consistently. Like a balm, it should be immediately targeted to a certain area, applied liberally, and then repeated.

In addition to everyday tasks and accomplishments, it can be used to reinforce incremental achievements on the way to realizing a final goal. This is especially true for project-oriented organizations but is relevant for every organization. A big project generally involves a series of smaller, interconnected jobs, and sometimes completing those can overwhelm the effort. Recognition along the way helps to steer people in the desired direction and keeps them on track. How can an employee know that he's on the right path if he doesn't get any feedback along the way?

Everyone in the organization should know exactly where they stand and how they are doing. This is all part of good communication and is a hallmark of effective management. People should never be forced to guess:

> *"My boss didn't yell at me today, I must be doing something right."*

Timing is a critical component of any recognition program. The more time that has elapsed between an achievement and its acknowledgment, the less the impact.

Immediacy is key. That is why the 20 Second Rule can be such a powerful tool. If it is used to continually reinforce good performance as often and as quickly as possible, the path to personal and organizational success is that much more attainable.

A manager for one of the big-box retailers was selected to open a new store. Anyone familiar with the size and scope of this kind of project, knows what a huge undertaking it is. One of the district managers made it a point to be involved in the employee recognition celebration the night before the grand opening. The ceremony, arranged to praise all those whose contributions helped to get the store ready, began when the new manager stepped up to address the crowd.

She looked out at all the faces and suddenly froze. A somewhat shocked look floated across her face, and then tears came to her eyes. There in the crowd was her brother who lived hundreds of miles away. The district manager contacted him and made an effort to get him to that pre-opening celebration.

That is a 20 second impact.

How do you think that store manager feels about all those people under her who worked so hard and about those people above her who showed her how much they cared? What is her performance going to look like going forward?

Obviously, the 20 second philosophy is not a one-off. It is an effective and integral component of good managerial technique and as such, it needs to be consistent and timely.

Specific recognition for a specific action within a specific time frame.

This means that your primary job in applying the rule requires paying attention--all the time! Getting to that 20 second impact takes work. It takes focus. In reality, it requires far more effort than you might like.

It takes much, much more than just 20 seconds. . .

"Management is doing things right; leadership is doing the right things." Peter Drucker, Objective Management Master

Recognition Rewards

Much has been written on recognition programs and policies. Some organizations go to great lengths to reward good performers and to demonstrate to the rest of the workforce the kind of work they deem valuable. Many of these programs are quite formal and often expensive--trips for top producers, a new car for a team leader, cash bonuses for the team. But it is often the simple rewards that people value the most. The money and the dream vacations are great, but there is something instinctively special about a personal moment of praise and recognition. It is universally satisfying. . .

Organizations should have formal recognition programs, but in addition to these, a consistent and very visible informal program practiced every day does so much to let people know that they are valuable members of the team. Once established and consistently adhered to, this kind of feedback becomes contagious. It starts to spread like a virus and begins to move in unexpected directions throughout the organization. It flows up as well as down, it crosses lines and departments, and it strengthens and grows as it moves. It becomes a metachronal wave.

"It is always the simple that produces the marvelous."
Amelia Barr, Morally Romantic Novelist

A tiny thing. . .

a speck of dust

a grain of sand

a parting whisper

can elicit something grand:

a newborn planet

a glistening pearl

a joyous heart

Something as small as the flutter of a
butterfly's wing can cause a typhoon
halfway around the world.
Chaos Theory

Change one small thing,
and you change everything. . .

A natural extension of the 20 Second Rule is to recognize people who recognize others. This is simply reinforcing the philosophy throughout the organization. Peers who praise peers in meetings, introducing good performers to other managers or groups, providing exposure opportunities for up-and-comers, even asking your boss to acknowledge someone on your team are examples of spreading the wealth. All this is extremely positive and it should be supported and encouraged. It's one brief moment out of the day that can pay an amazing dividend.

I see you

"I just wanted to take a sec to thank you for continuing to inspire me! It may sound corny, but I took to heart your "20 Second Rule". After pondering it for a while on my flight home, I thought to myself, "I think I do a pretty good job already with my associates. Would this be any more of a benefit?" Let me tell you, IT WAS! By actively dedicating even that small amount of time to communicating with my associates, I have been able to build an even stronger team. I feel that it has been easier to communicate and get buy-in from them, it's helped me grow as a leader, and has just been an overall success. So, Thank You for giving me a great tool to put in my tool belt that I am certain I will never forget!" Email to HR Director from Front-line Manager.

Although the 20 Second Rule is aimed at recognizing and inspiring good performance, it doesn't always have to be performance related. Sometimes recognition is as simple as treating people well, as fellow human beings.

Everyone you work with is worth it.

A district manager for a large retail company received a fancy, branded NASCAR jacket at an annual event. A few weeks later the manager was visiting one of her stores for a meeting. Sporting the jacket, she mingled with several front-line employees, and one of them approached her. The employee told the manager what a huge NASCAR fan she was and how much she admired that jacket.

Everyone assembled for the meeting and the manager stepped up to address them. The very first thing she did was call up the employee who liked her jacket. She took it off and simply gave it to her.

The district manager didn't think much more about that event until about 10 years later, when a location manager who had been in attendance that day as a relatively new hire, ran into her. He told her that employees still talk about that gesture, and that he will personally never forget the impact it had on everyone in that meeting. Ten years later. . .

I will never forget what you said...

what you did...

how I felt...

A PLAN OF ACTION

Most good leaders recognize the value of daily, positive interactions. A general atmosphere of camaraderie and spirited competition lift the morale of everyone and inspire people to perform at their best. And it can be accomplished in a very short amount of time. If you haven't given much thought about the brief interactions you have with your employees and peers, you're missing one of the most consistent and valuable opportunities you have as a manager. Think about it, you get a hundred chances a day to:

Praise

Acknowledge

Enable

Motivate

One hundred chances a day!

At 20 seconds a pop, that's approximately one half hour out of your busy day. A half an hour a day to completely remake and/or rejuvenate an entire organization. And it starts with just 20 seconds.

Here are some very simple things you can do to begin embracing the 20 second philosophy:

Take note of small things that please you when you walk through a department.

Balance the negative things you see with positive ones. Give the positive more weight in your mind.

For every negative issue you come across, look for two positive issues.

Tell people how good you feel about something they do right.

Thank people often.

Encourage everyone, not just those who are struggling.

Speak to someone you haven't spoken to in a long time.

Seek out people that you don't know in your area of responsibility.

Practice a little positive disruption.

Make an effort to meet everyone on your team, even if it takes weeks.

Learn people's names and use them as much as possible.

Adopt the practice of praising people without any hidden agenda.

Use a combination of private, personal praise and very open, public instances of recognition.

Occasionally find something un-work related to praise.

When you're addressing sub-par performance issues, even minor ones, do it privately, behind closed doors.

Encourage people to recognize their peers.

Ask someone's opinion and thank them for their perspective.

Introduce strong performers to other managers or groups.

Briefly single out individual contributions in meetings and informal gatherings.

Ask your boss to acknowledge someone on your team.

Emphasize success rather than failure. Celebrate it.

Be timely with your praise or recognition.

Use the organization's grapevine or informal lines of communication to distribute positive comments about others.

Put up a bulletin board where everyone can post something positive about anyone else--high or low--in the organization.

Purchase a set of Thank You cards, write something personal, and surprise people with them.

In large organizations, use emails as a way to recognize and thank people; make them brief but specific and personal. CC peers and other leaders.

Be open and transparent. Don't be afraid to let people see your faults, particularly if you can laugh at them.

Lead by being human.

Tick tock...

Do you know what the secret of life is?
No. What?
This...
Your finger?
One thing. Just one thing. You stick to that, and everything
else don't mean (squat).
That's great. But what's the one thing?
That's what you gotta figure out...

Mitch and Curly, City Slickers

Is there a secret to effective management? Is there one thing that will enable you to get the results you want? If you think about it seriously, you come to understand that it isn't that simple. Different situations require different responses. One standardized approach applied to something as complex as people management just doesn't cut it. But if forced to boil it down to something as simple as one thing, it would be this:

Your Management Tool Box

It's all the tools you have acquired along that journey we call a career. Your training, your experience, all the lumps you've taken, form the box which contain those tools. The secret to success, of course, is knowing how and when to use them.

*"The expectations of life depend upon diligence;
the mechanic that would perfect his work
must first sharpen his tools."
Confucius, Philosophical Ethicist*

Some of the best tools ever devised are the simplest. Take the chisel. It's been around for thousands of years and it hasn't changed much. It's clean, sleek, and intuitively easy to use. But not everyone can take a chisel to a block of marble and create something amazing. That takes years of dedicated effort. Yet with practice the tool becomes familiar, easier to use, and eventually a part of you. Success in all endeavors depends on how well you use the tools at your disposal.

The 20 Second Rule is just another tool. It's clean, it's simple, it's intuitively easy to use. And like the chisel, in the right hands it can produce a masterpiece. . .

Tick tock. . .

Between them, Neal and Alisa Grandy have over fifty years of managerial experience. In diverse corporate cultures and through various entrepreneurial pursuits, they have acquired an insightful perspective on successful leadership, sound management practices, and effective employee motivation.

Contact them at:
acaciallc@comcast.net

Printed in Germany
by Amazon Distribution
GmbH, Leipzig

29138899R00052